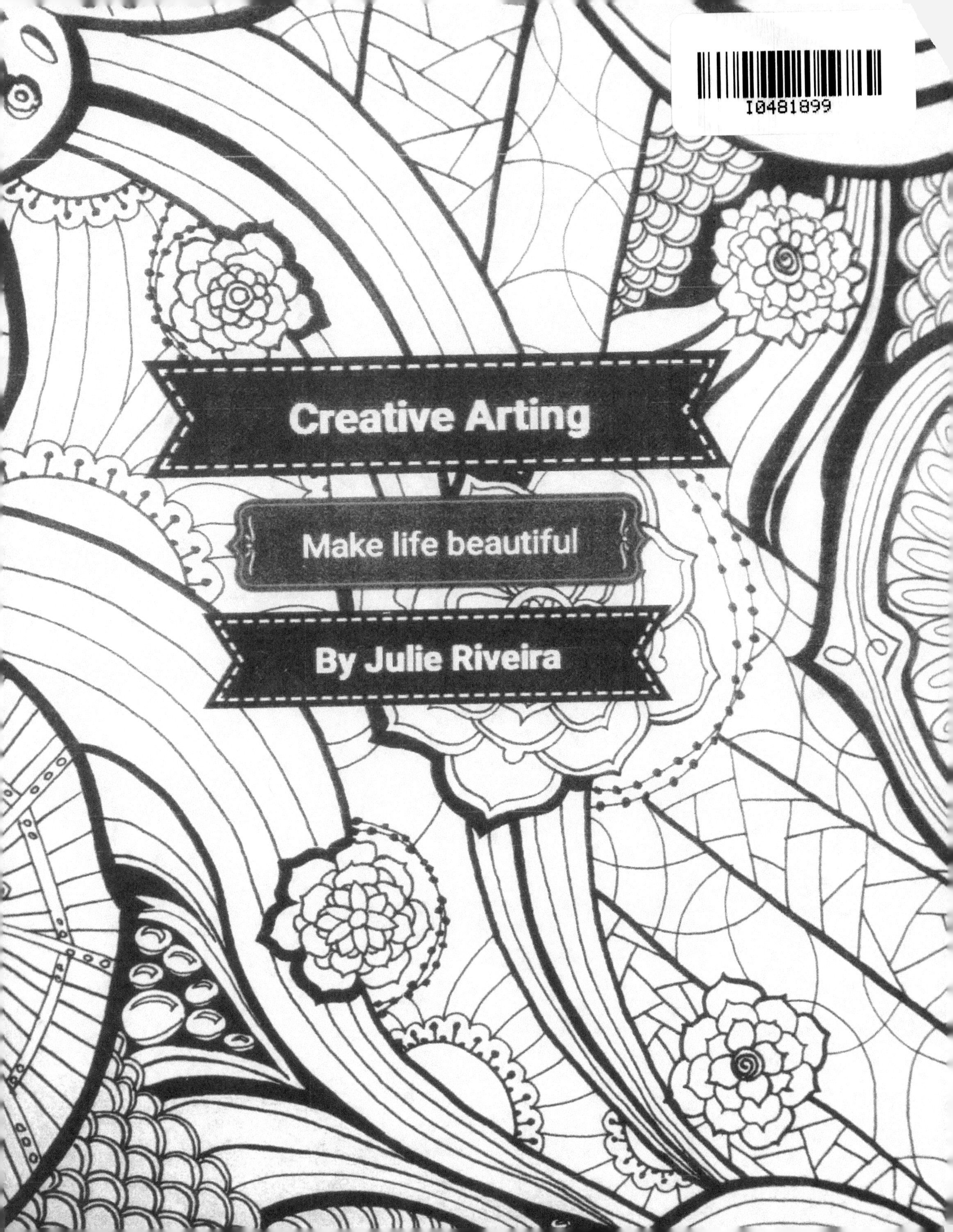

Creative Arting

Make life beautiful

By Julie Riveira

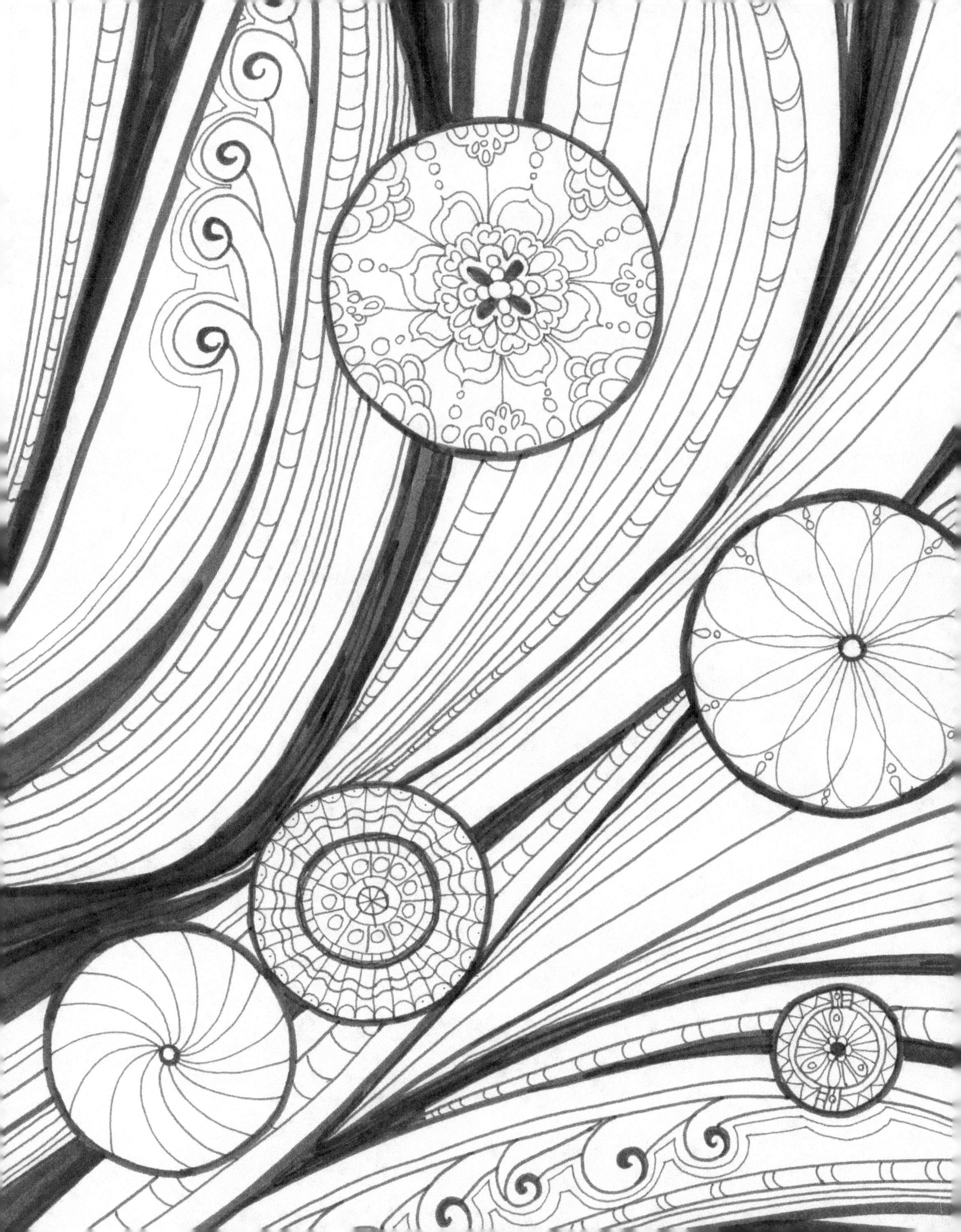

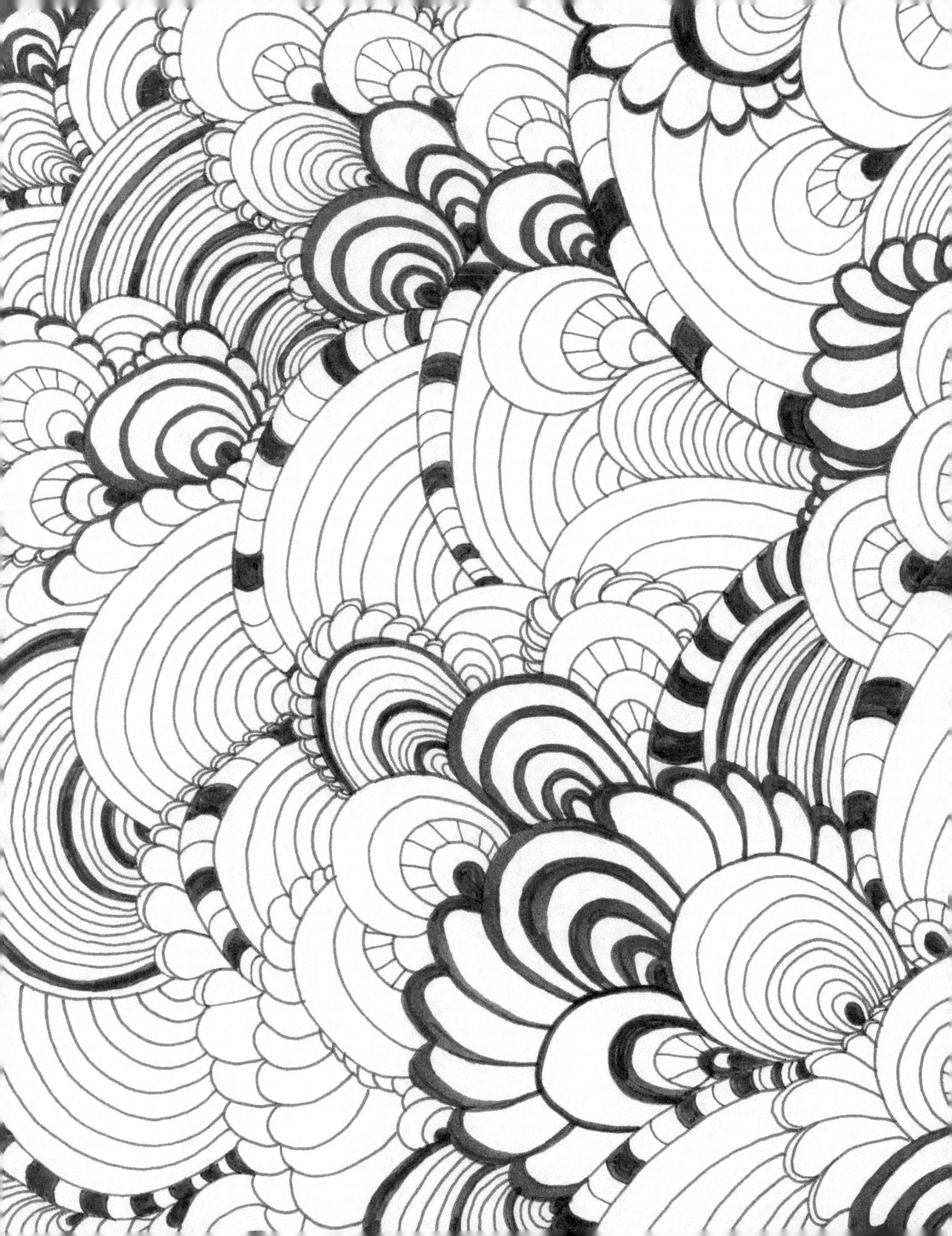

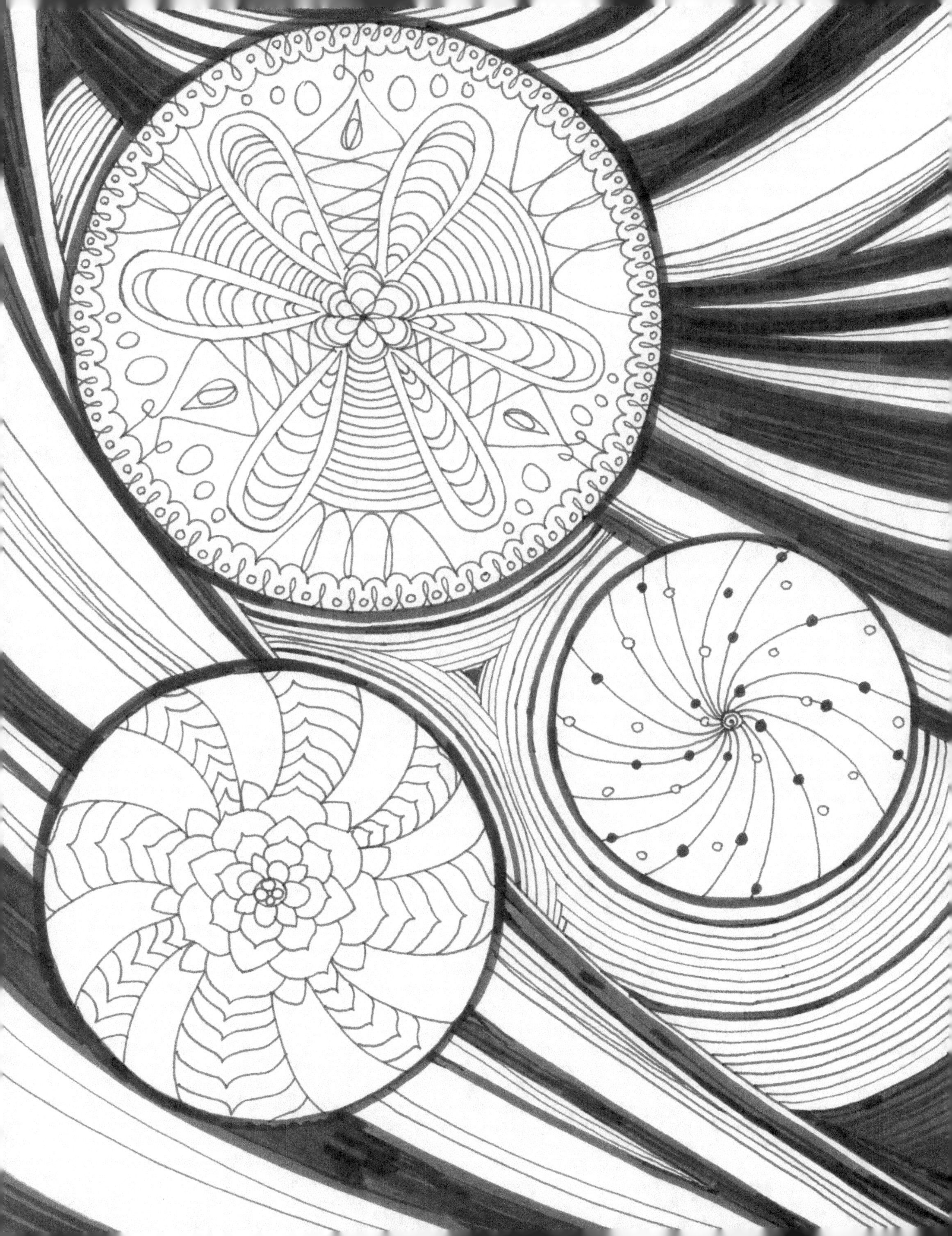

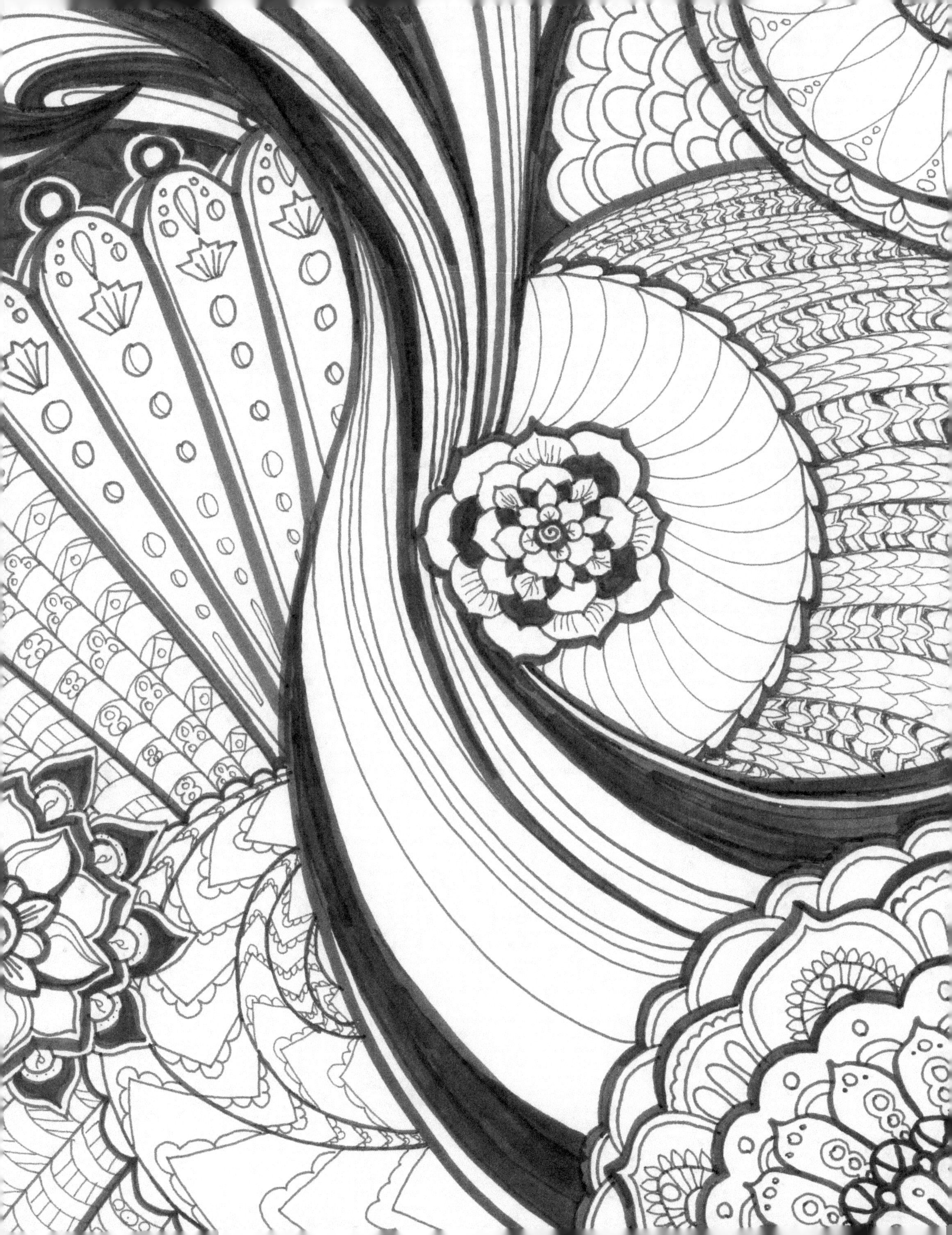

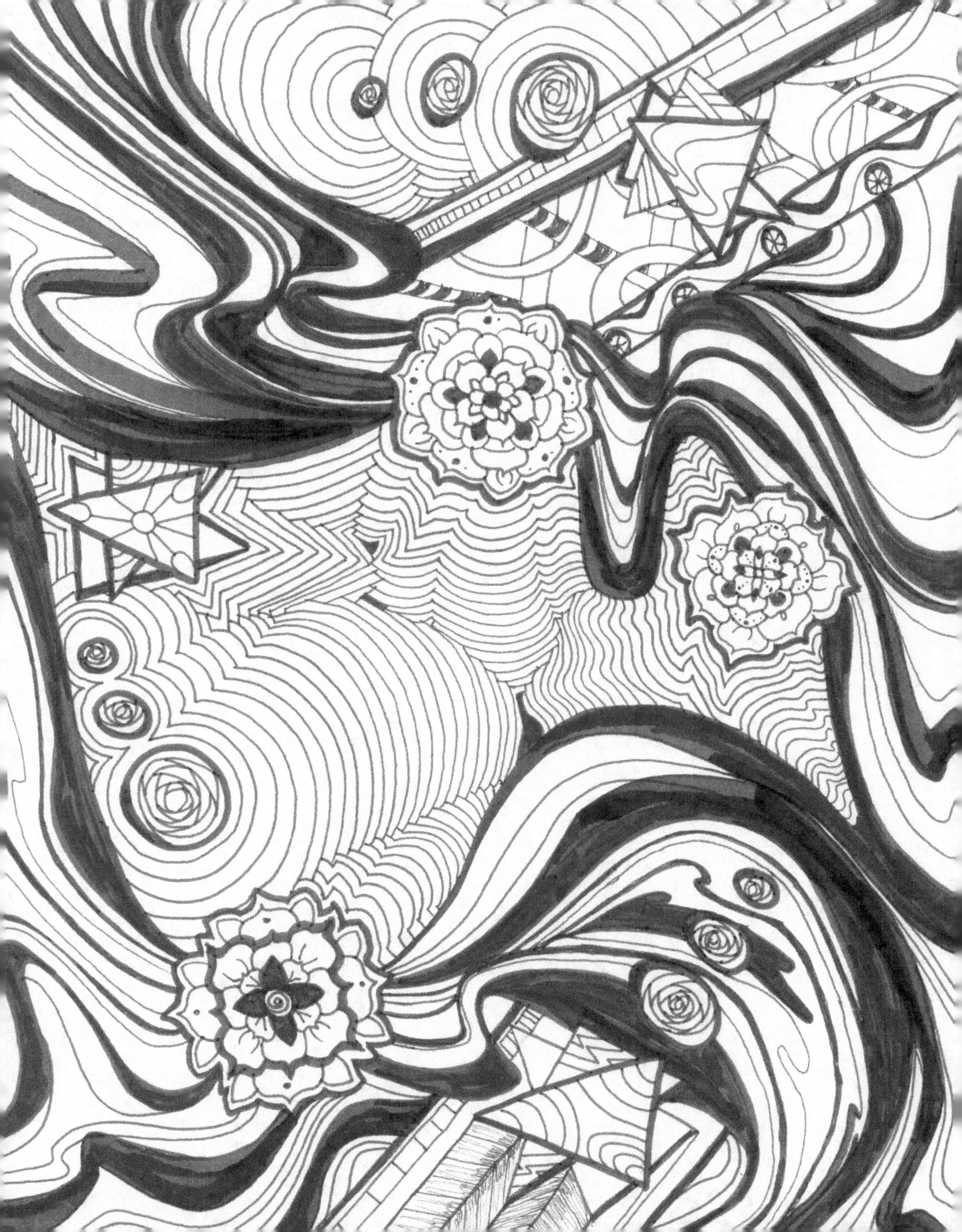

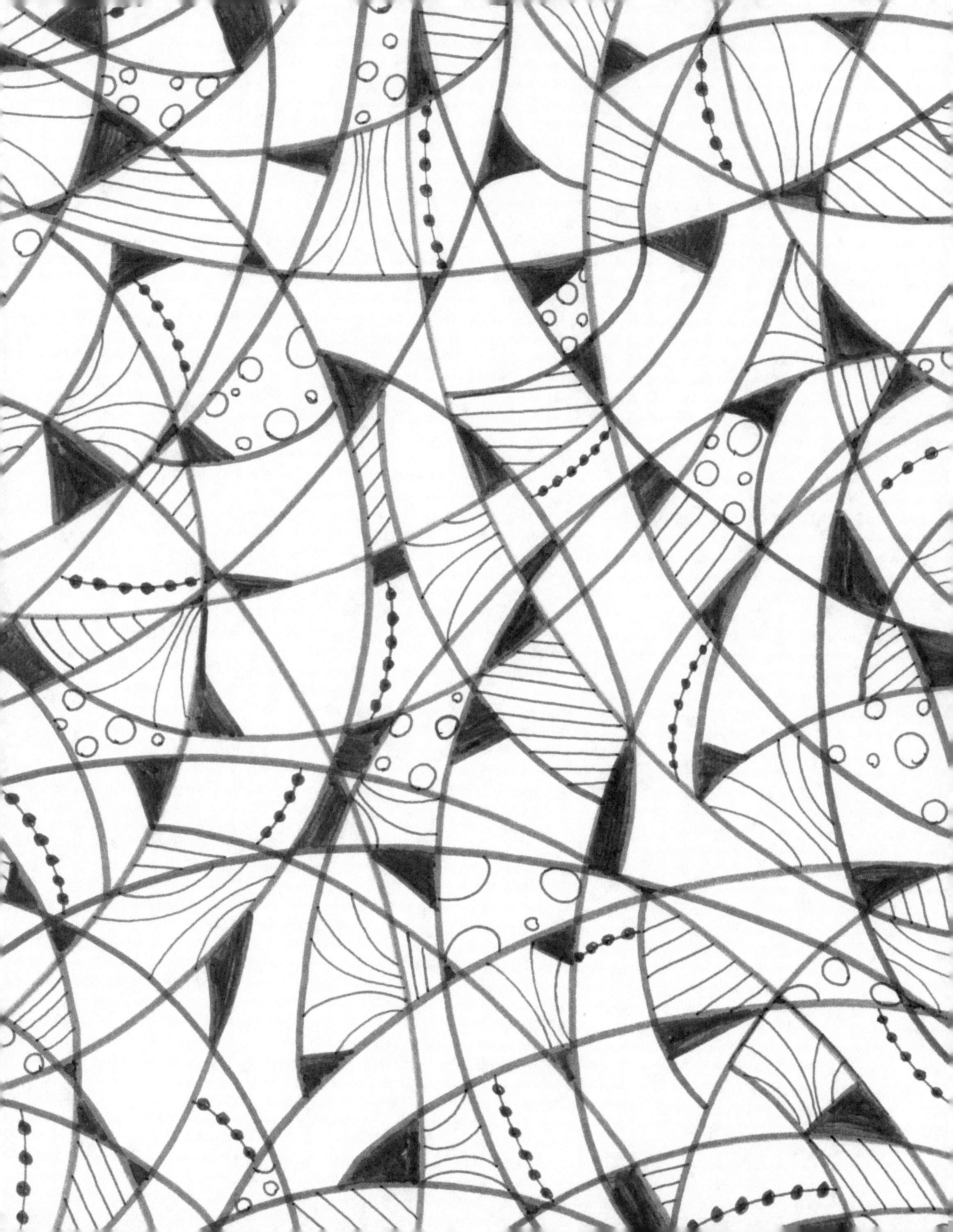

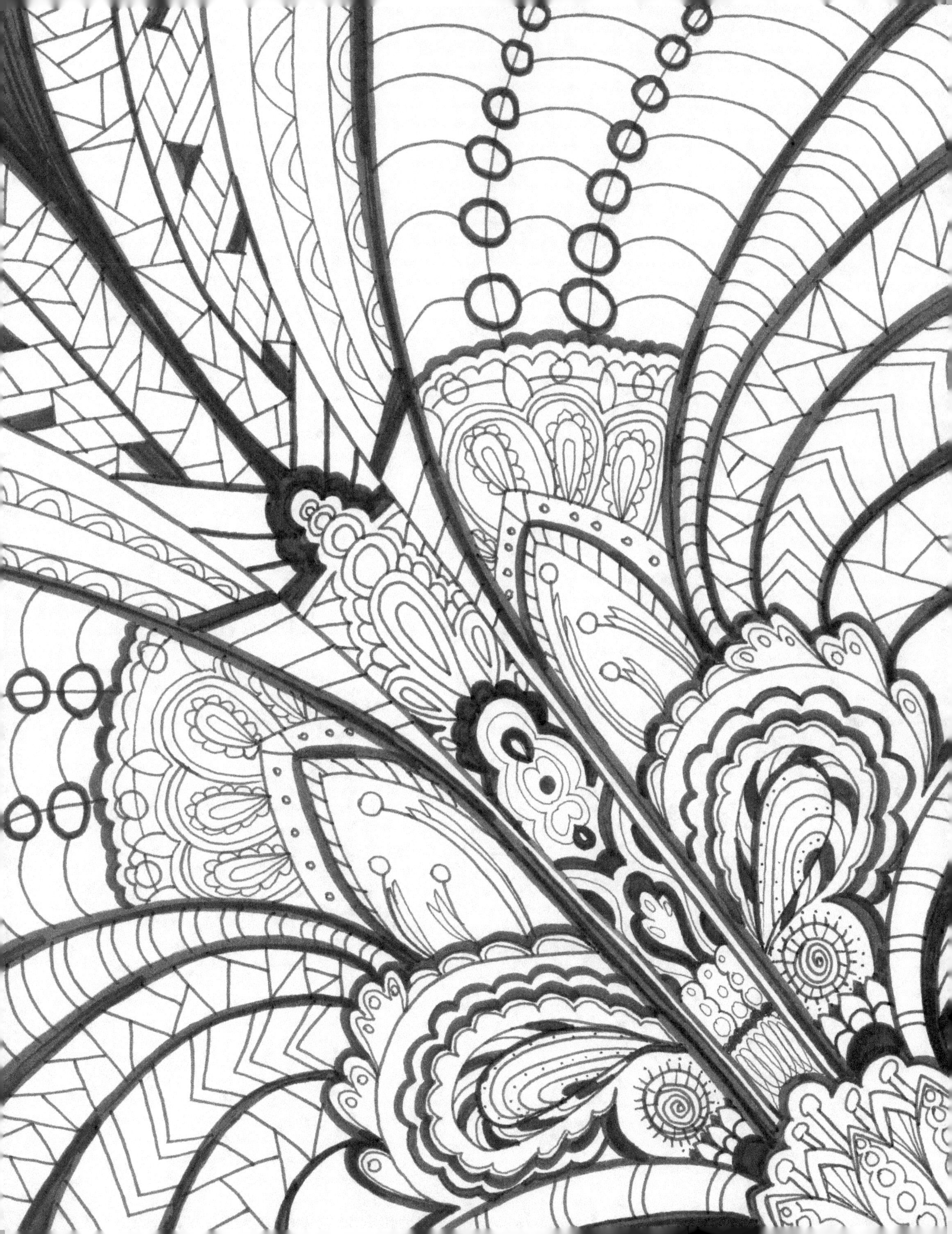

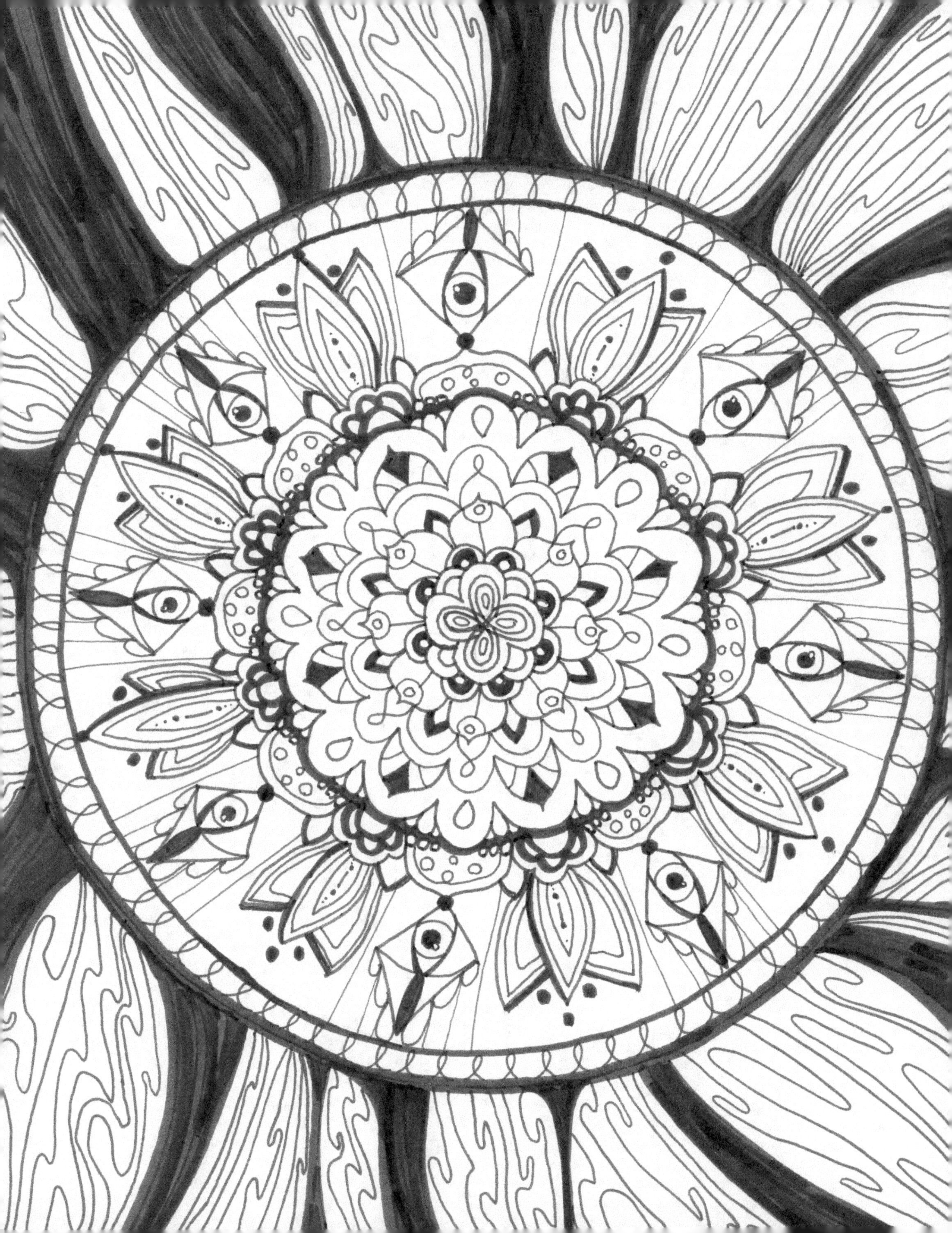

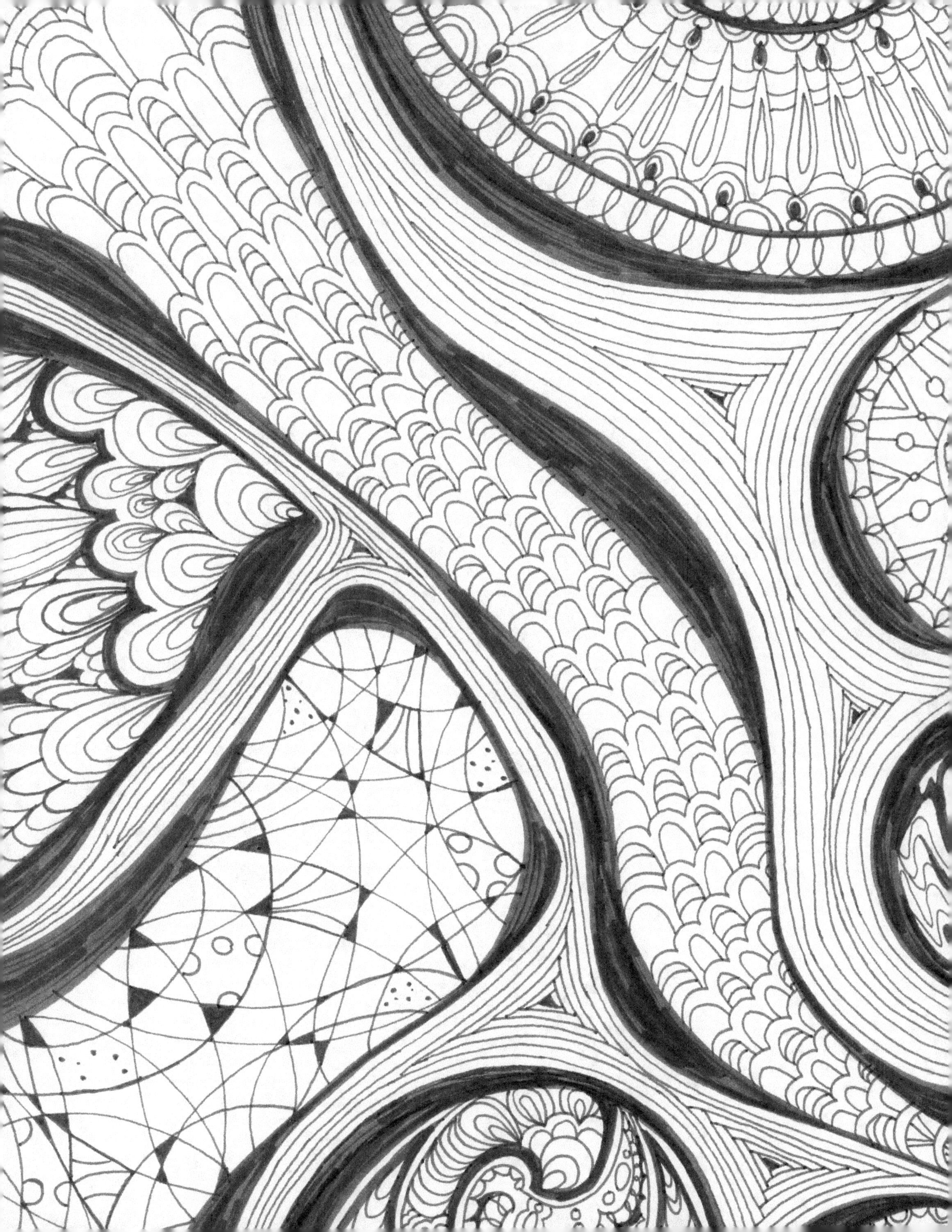

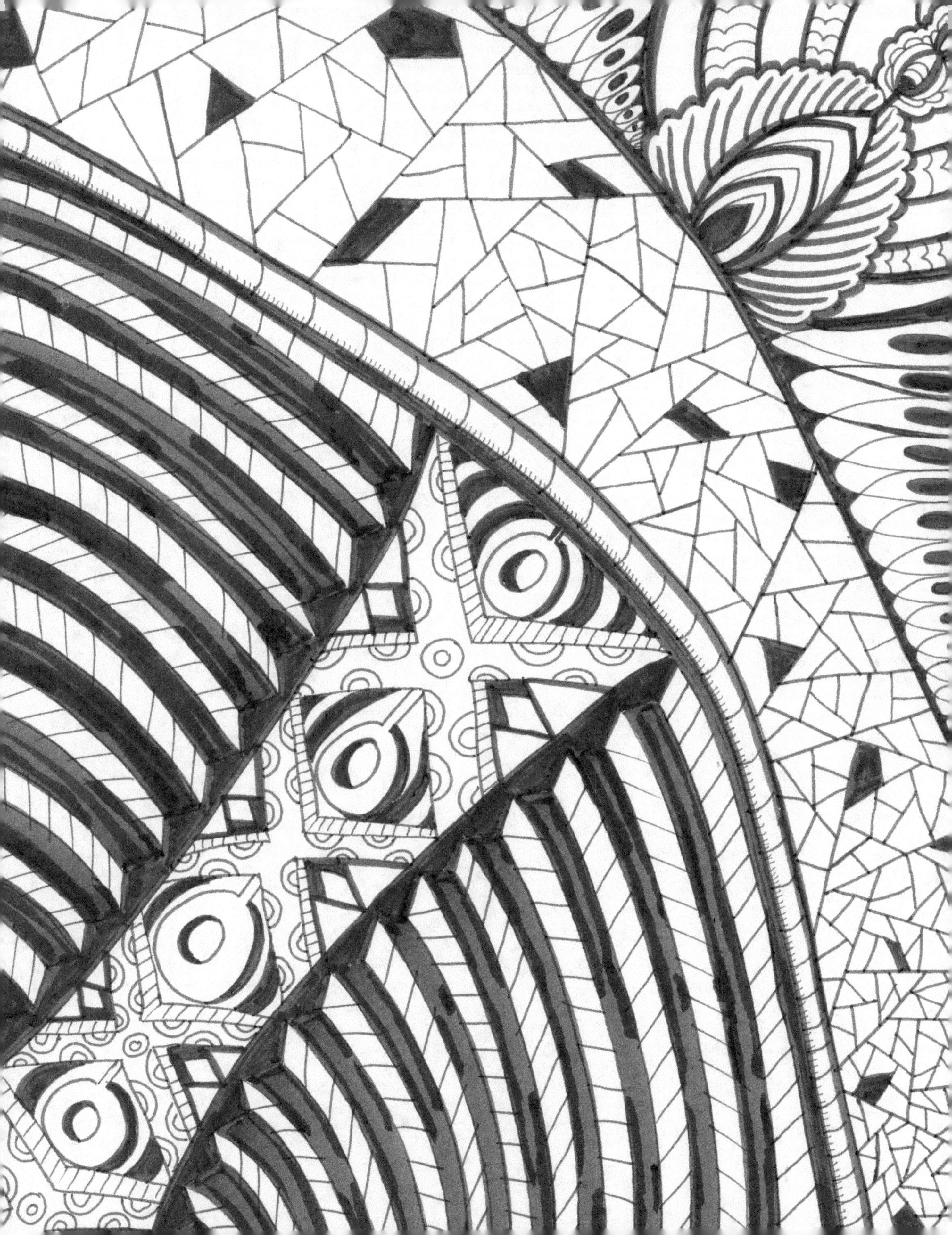

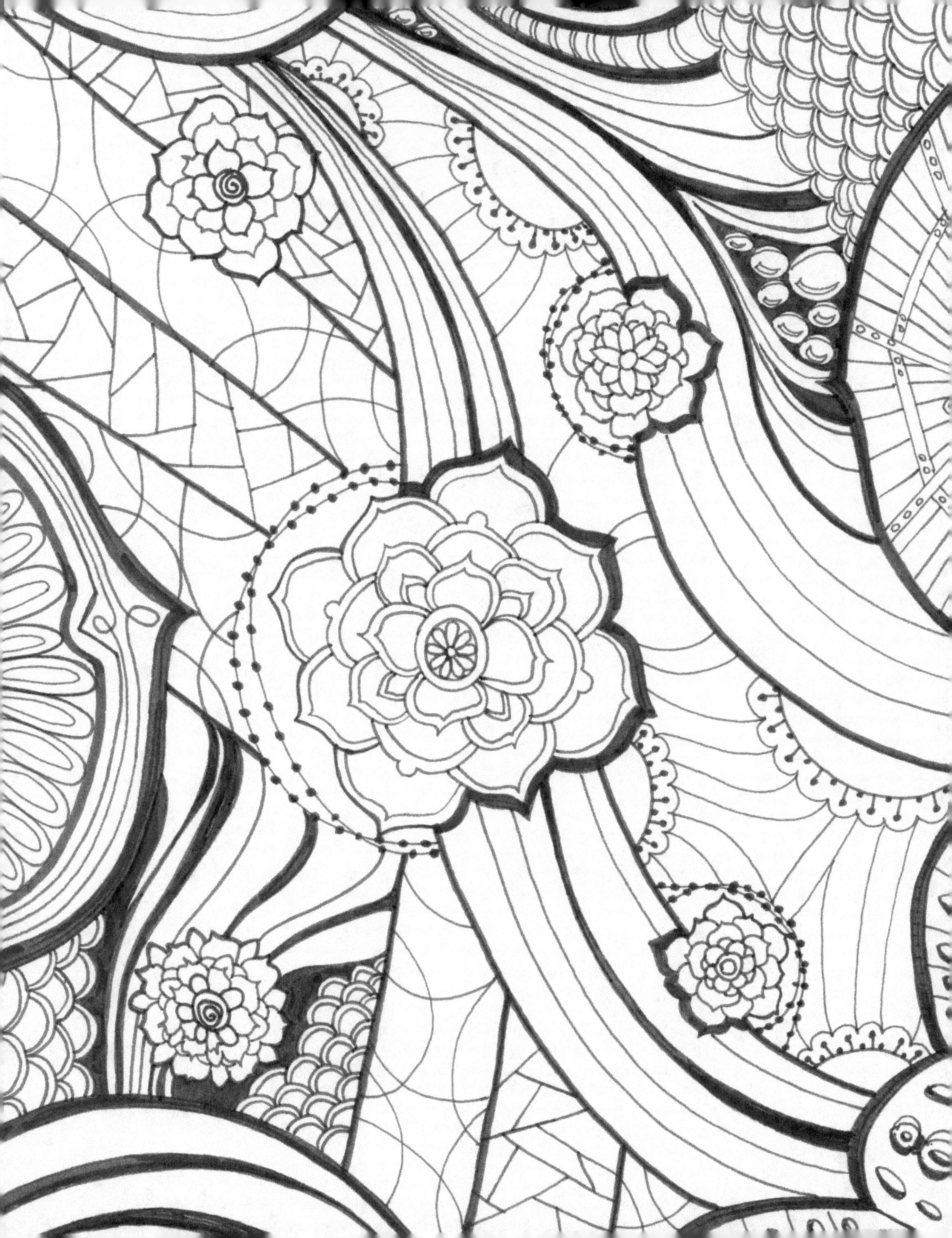

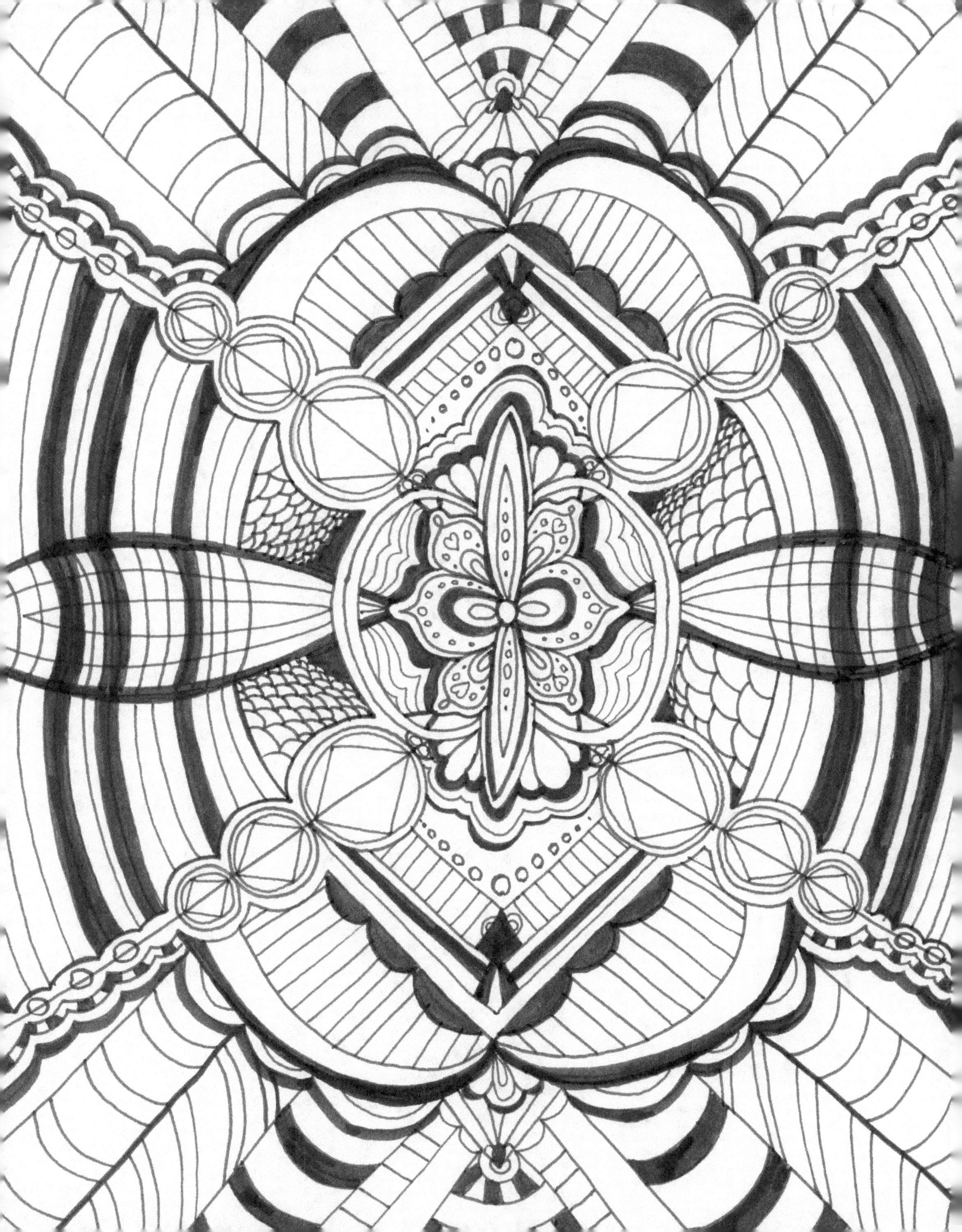

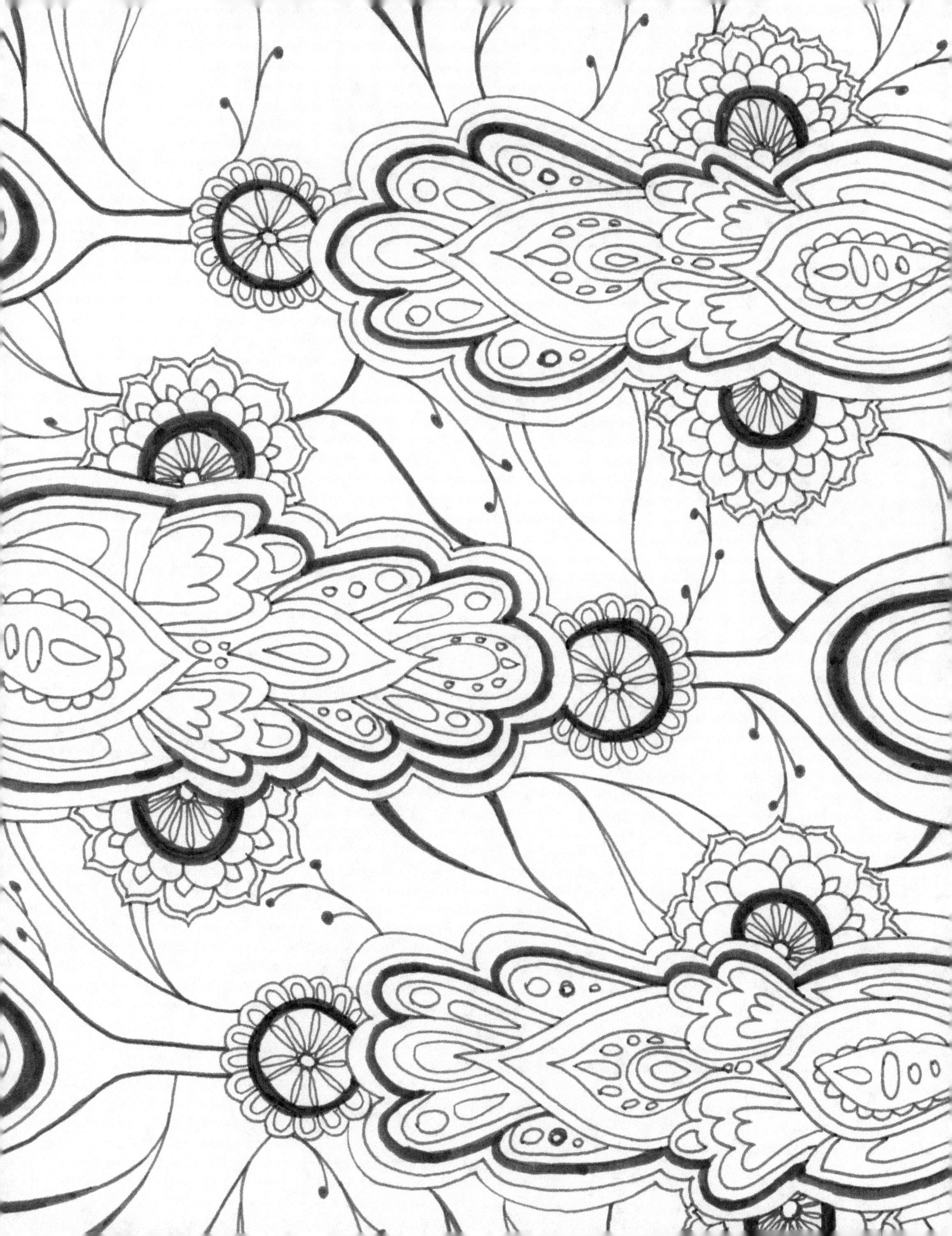

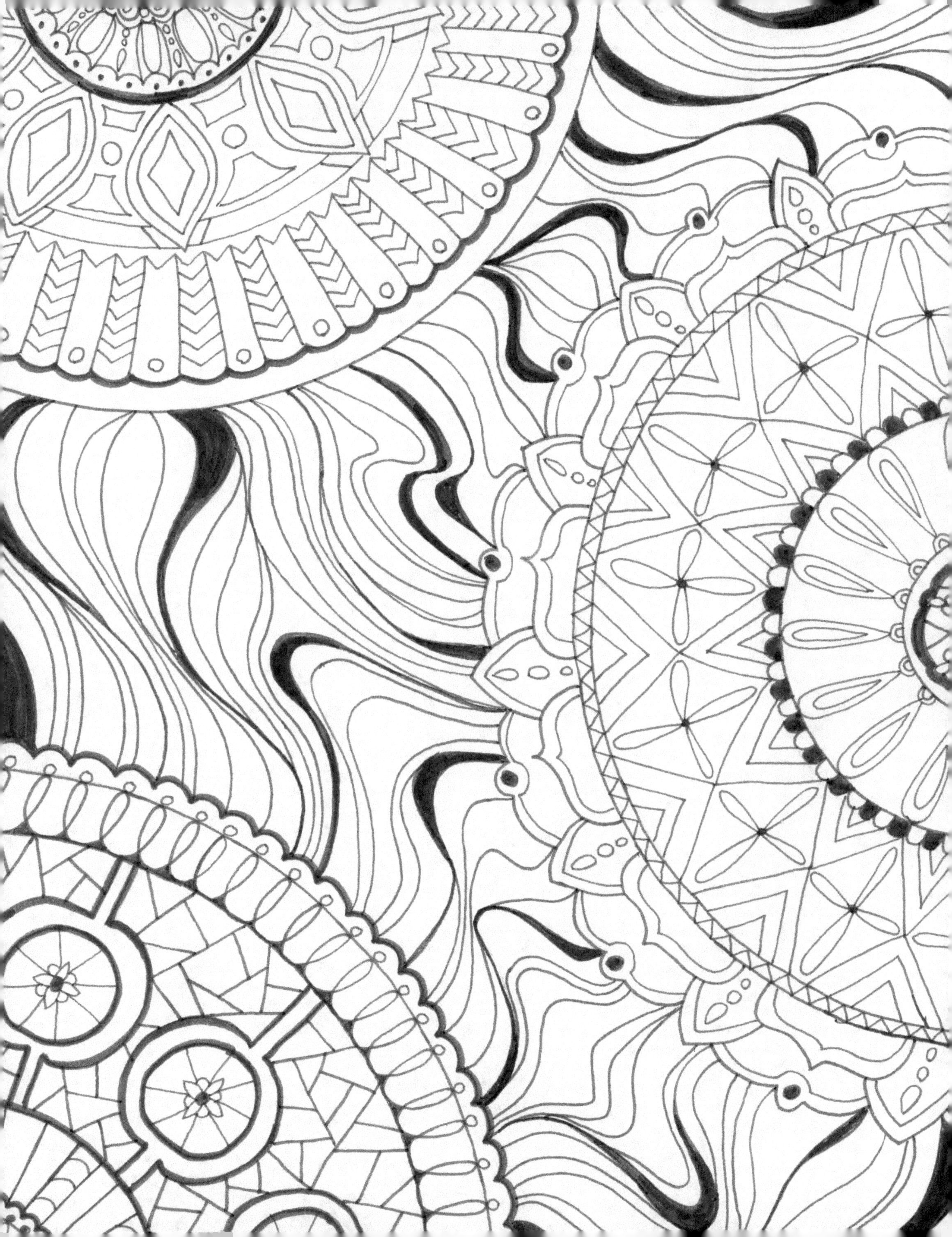

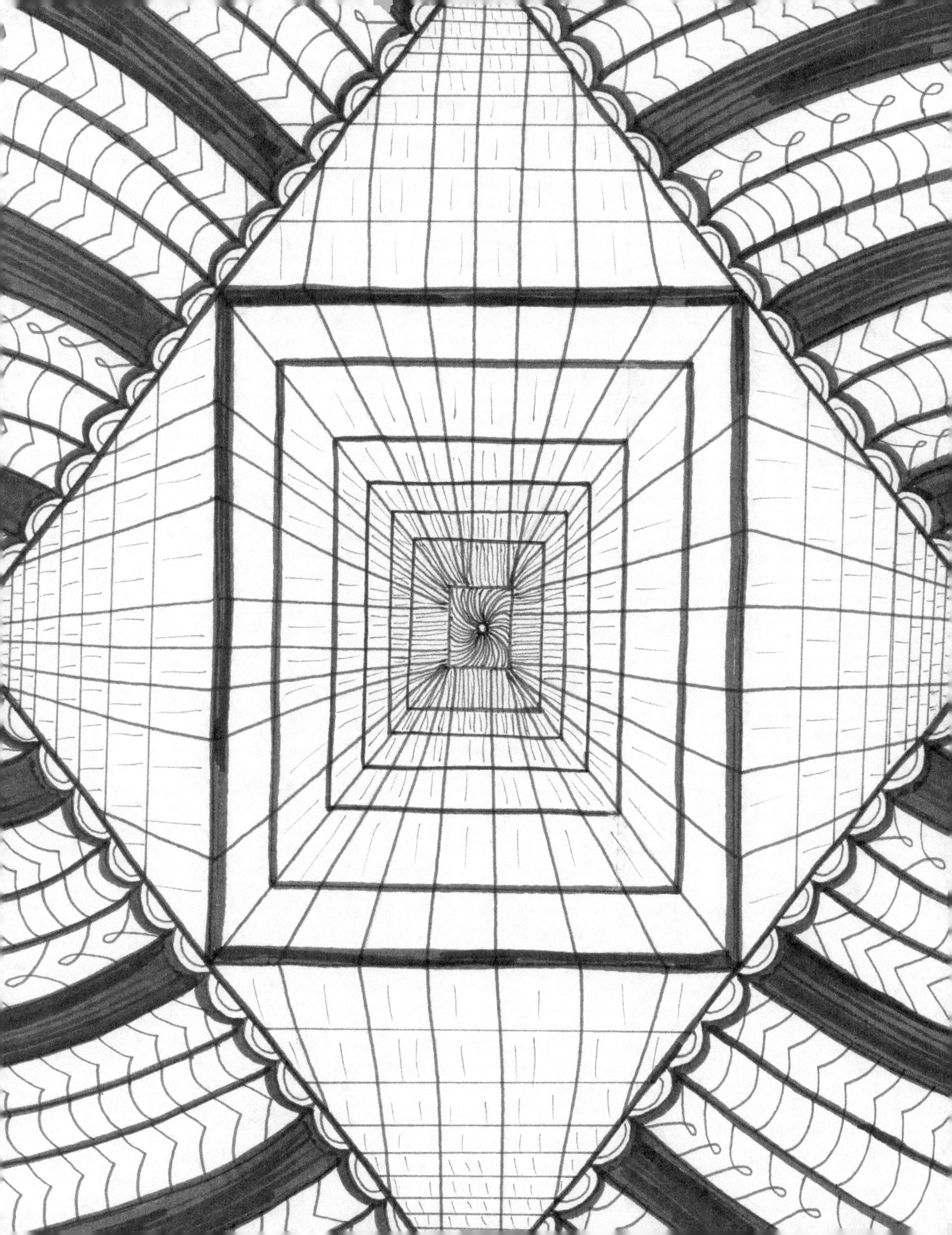

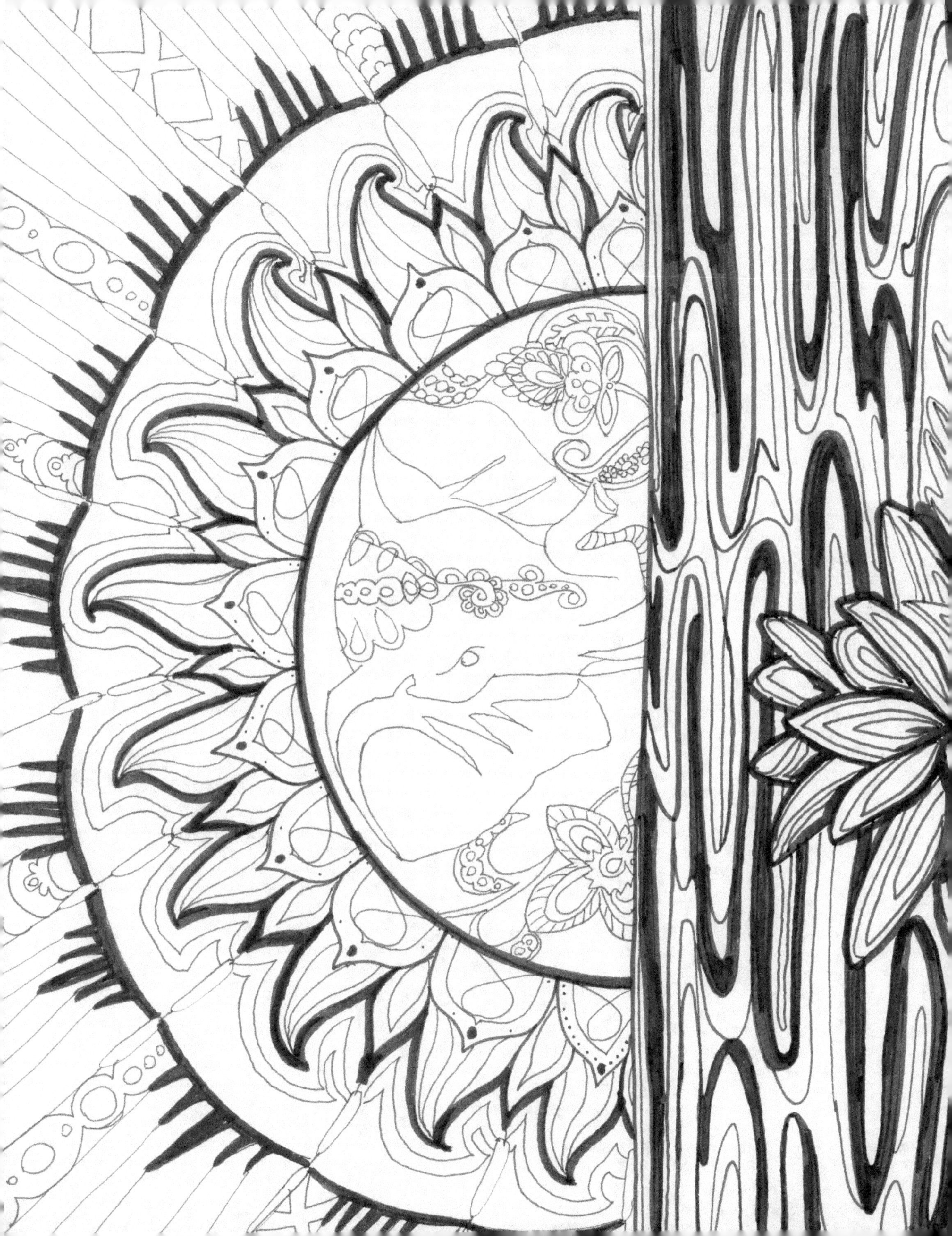

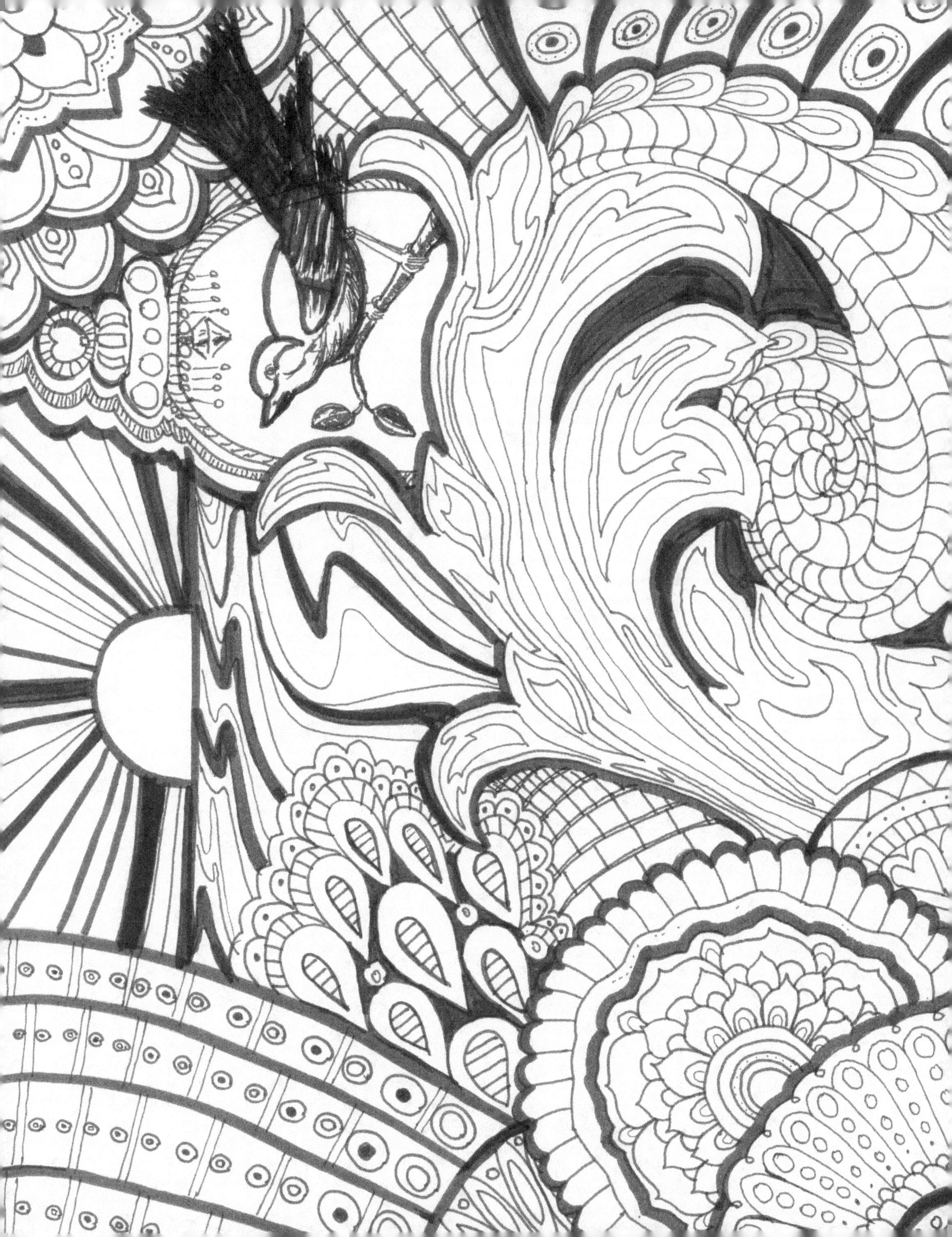

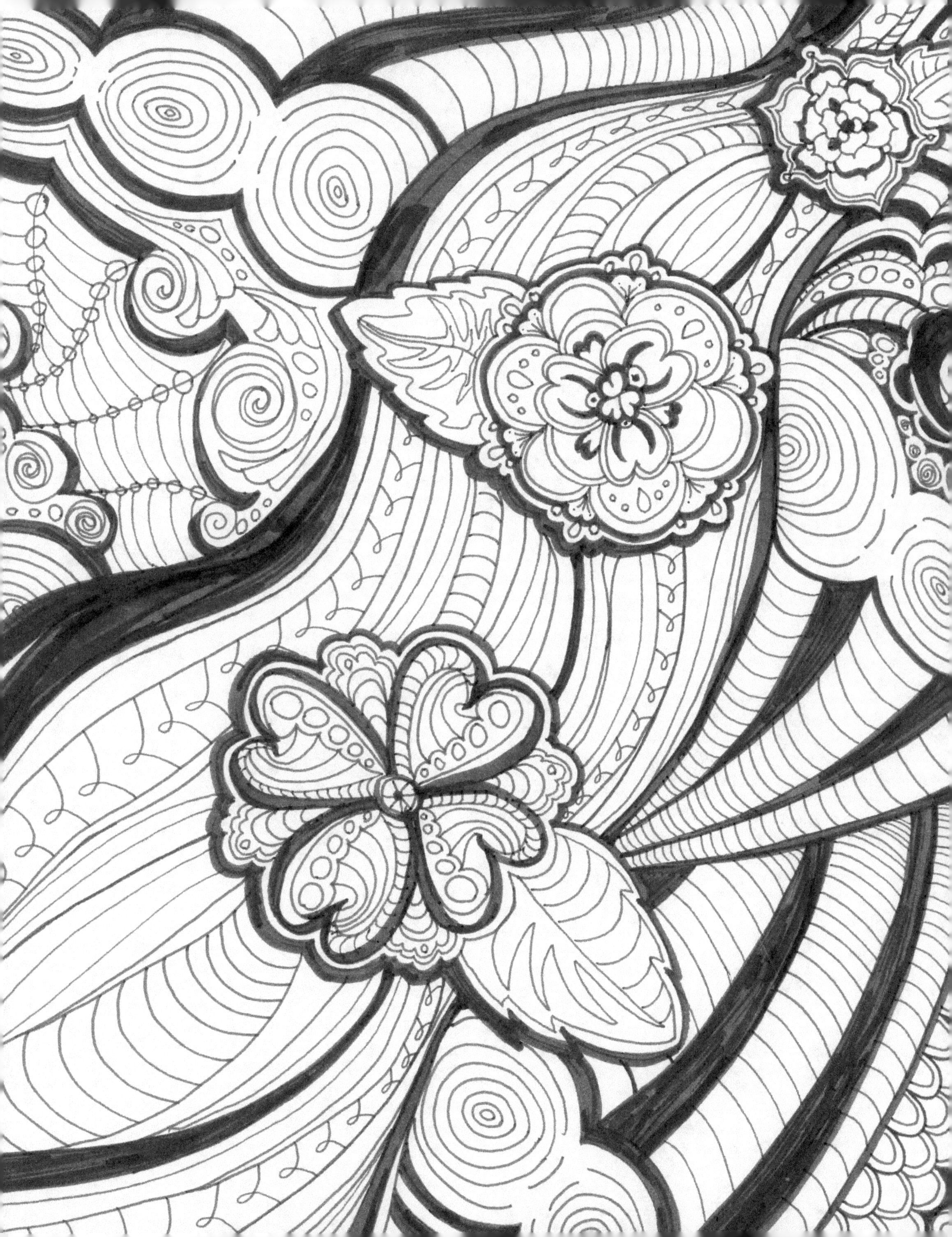

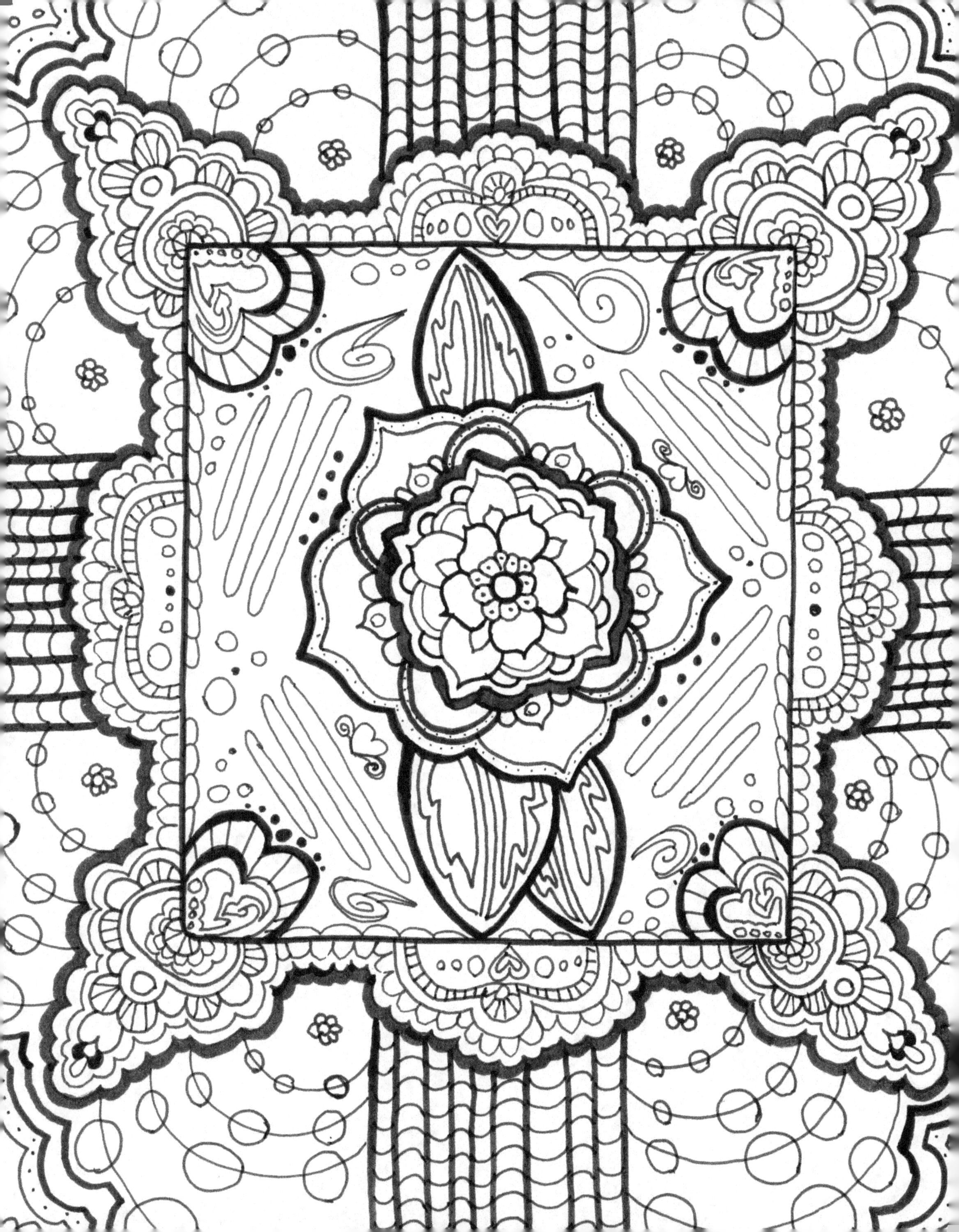

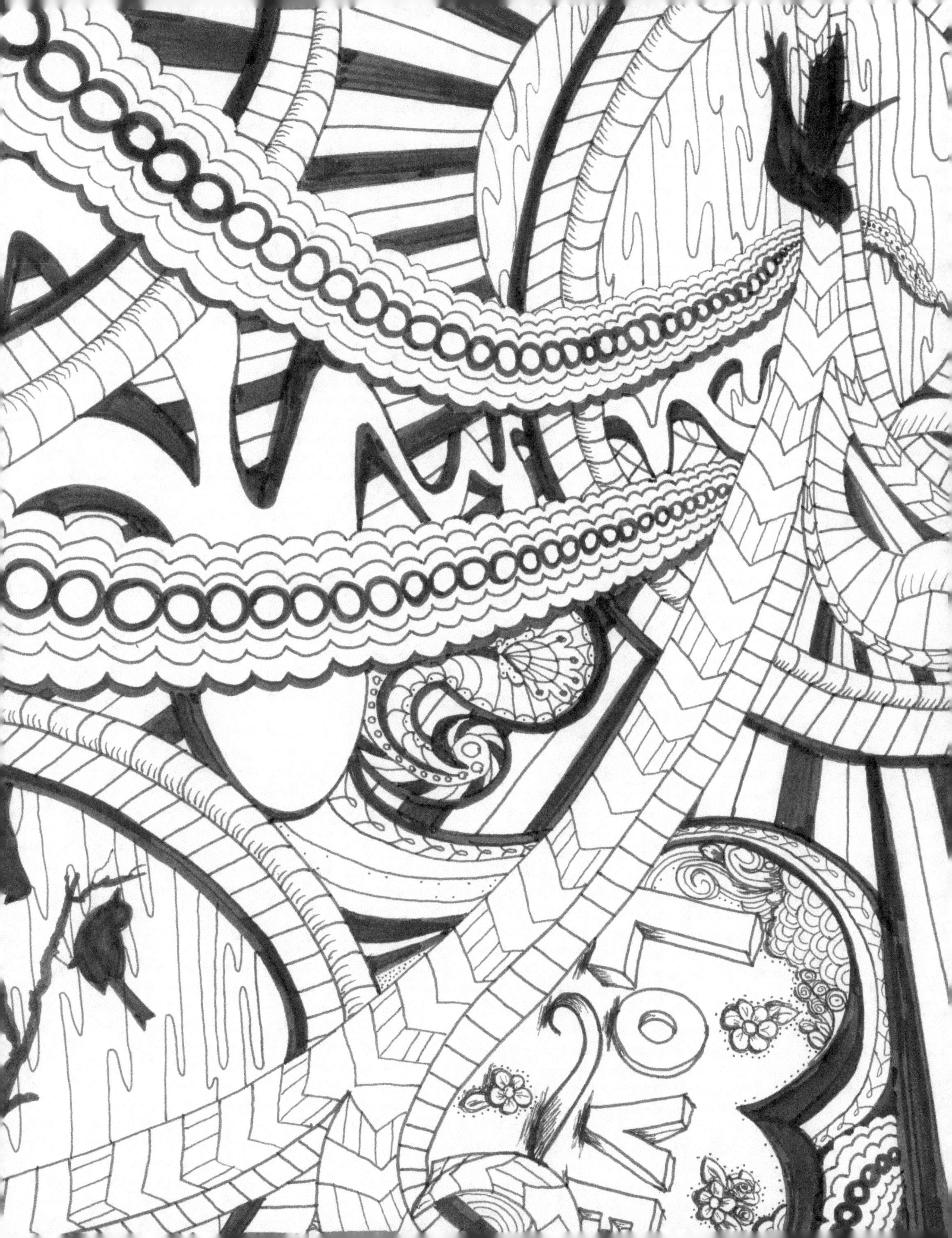

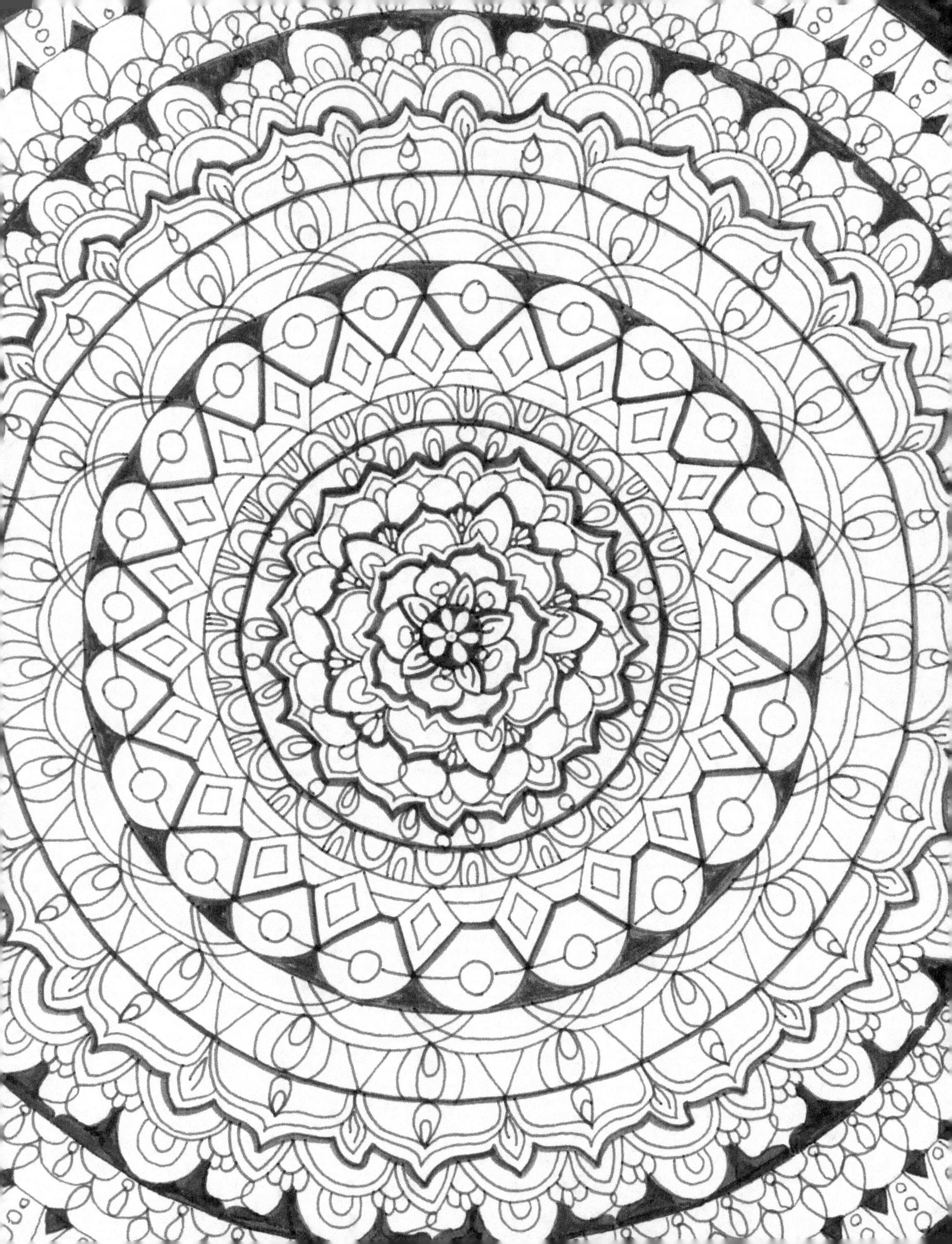

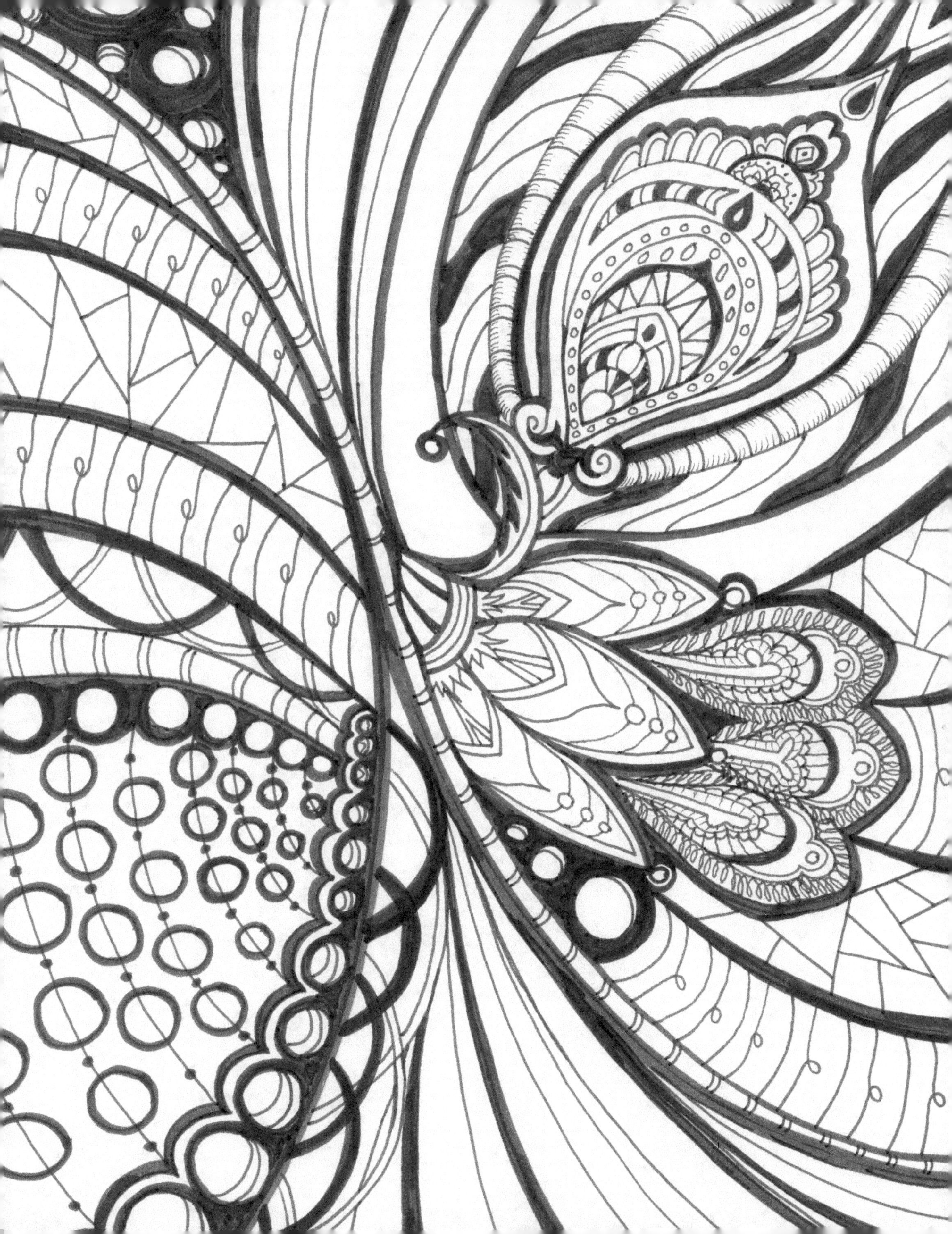

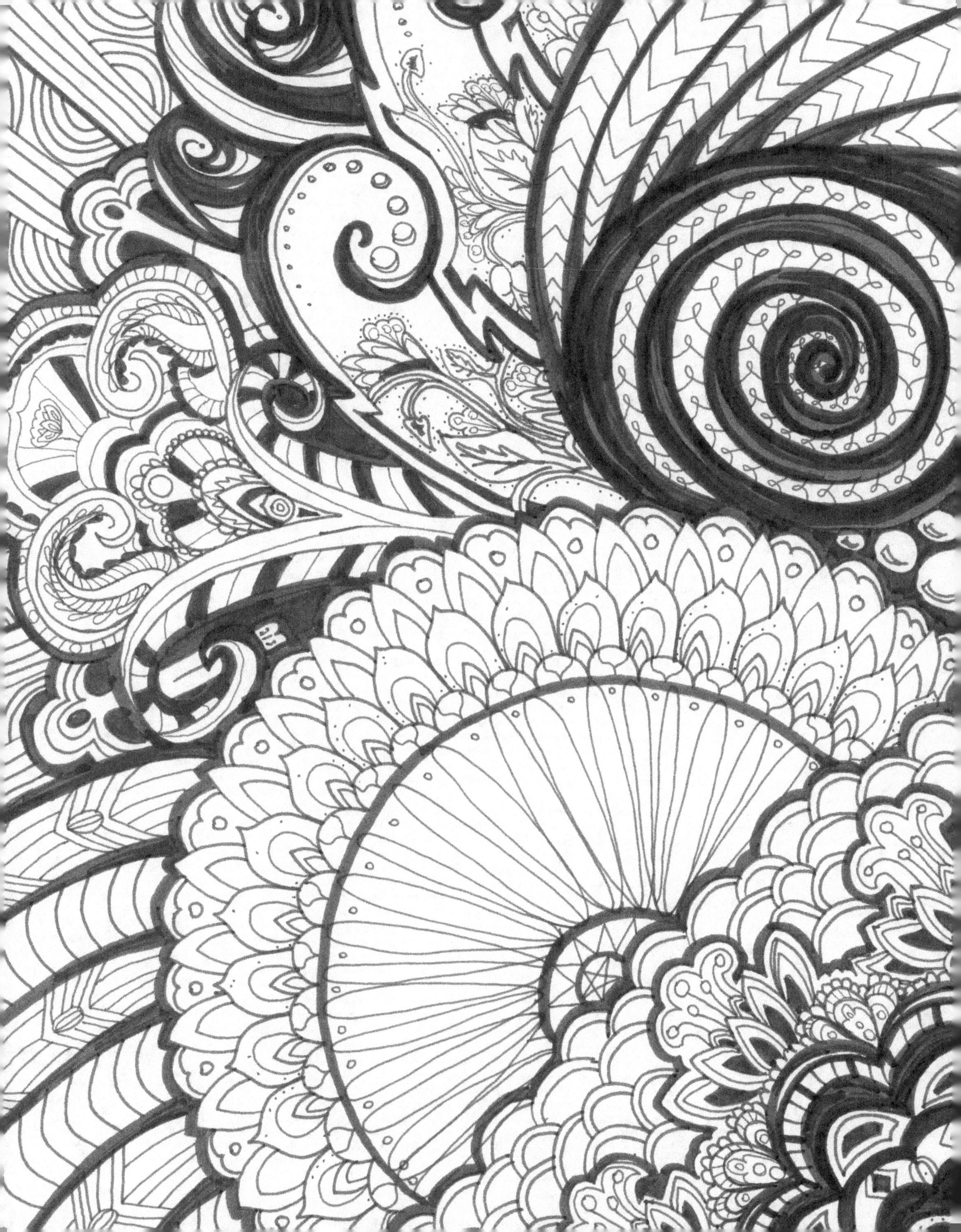

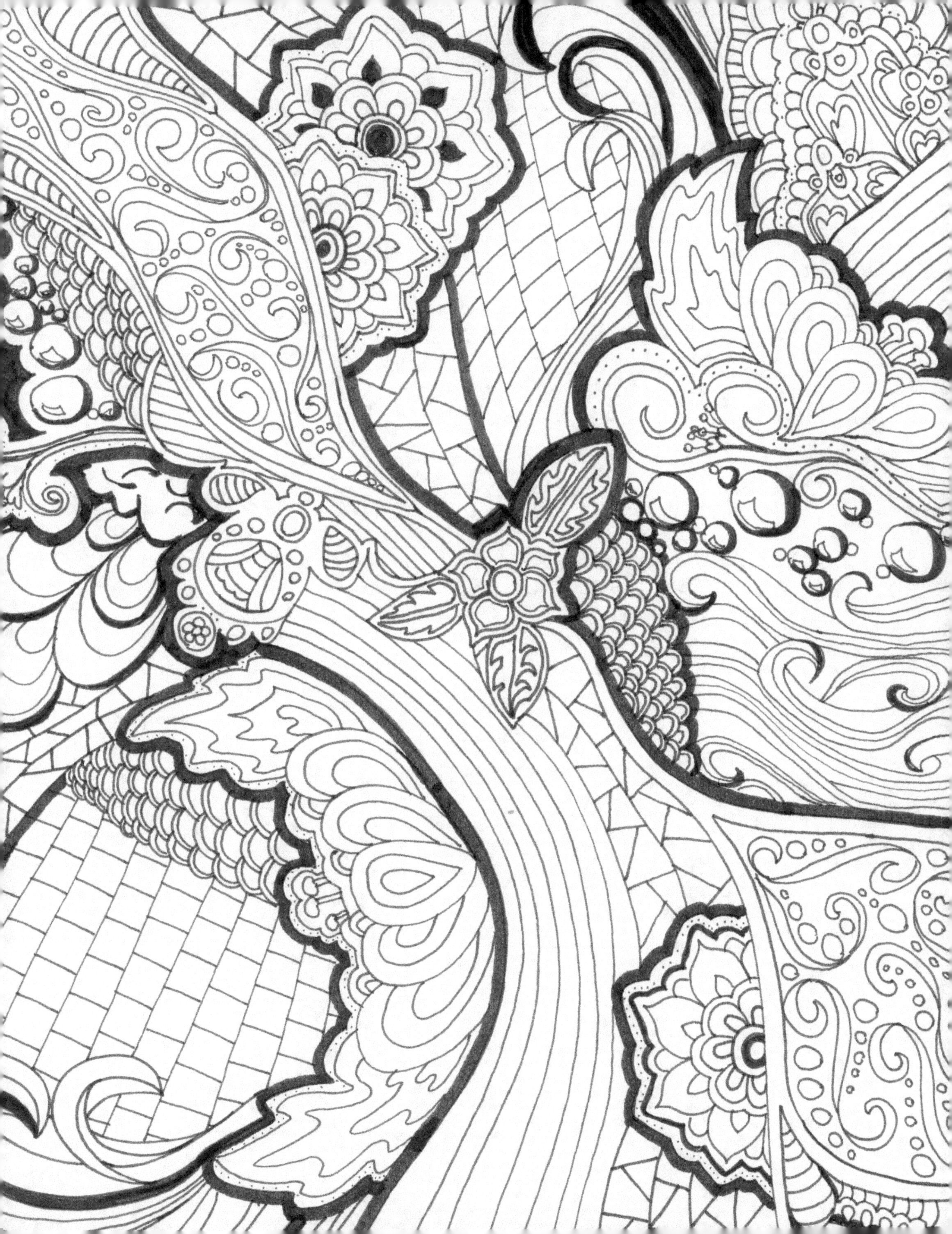

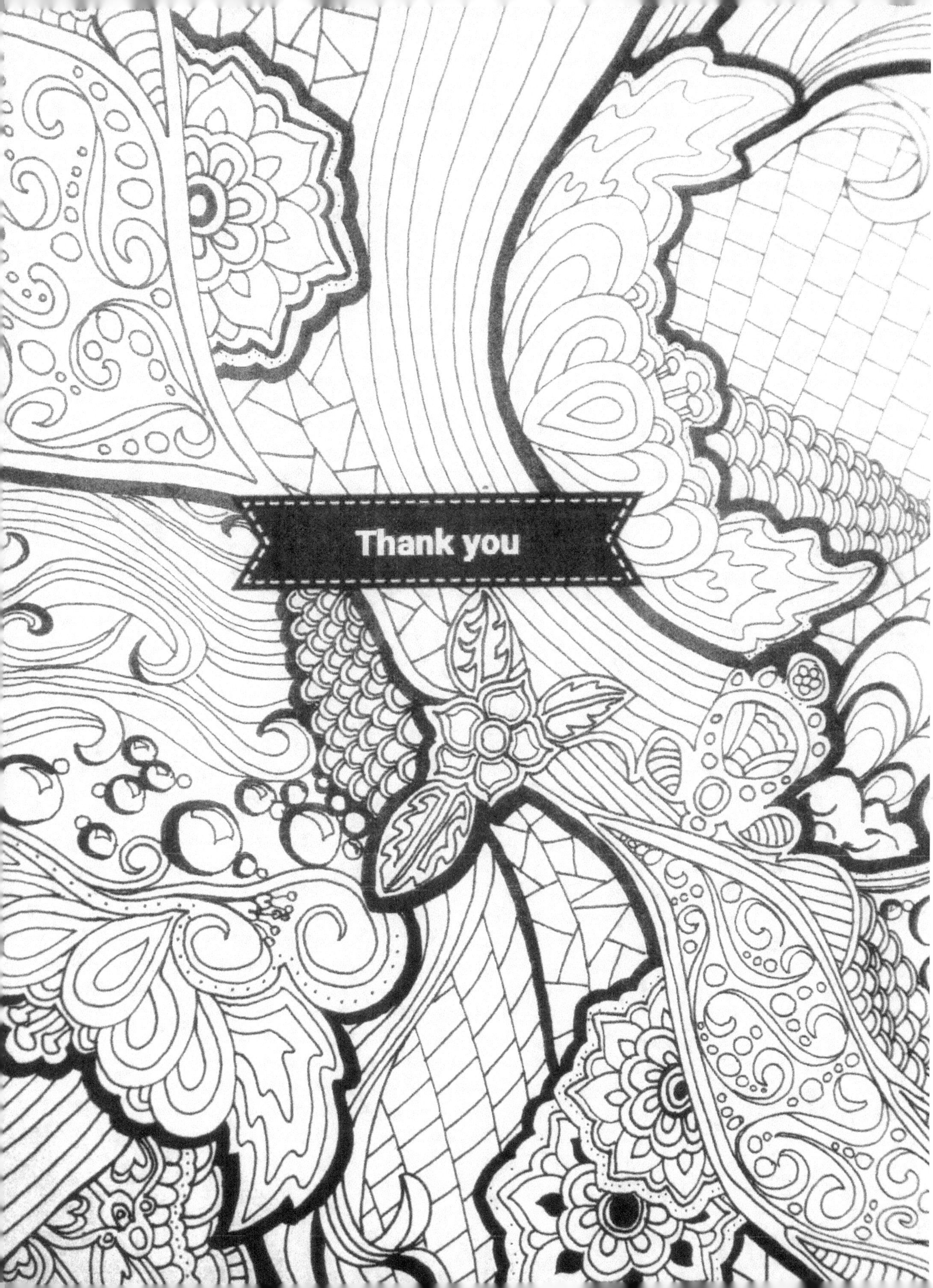
Thank you

www.ingramcontent.com/pod-product-compliance
Lightning Source LLC
Chambersburg PA
CBHW081640220526
45468CB00009B/2506
* 9 7 8 1 9 8 1 6 1 8 7 1 2 *